Principles FOR LIFE CHANGE

A Handbook for Biblical Application

GENESIS - DEUTERONOMY

PASTOR BILL HILL
PASTOR DENNIS L. HORNE

A Handbook for Biblical Application

PRINCIPLES FOR LIFE CHANGE
Genesis - Deuteronomy
©2004 by Pastor Bill Hill & Pastor Dennis L. Horne

Published by FOCUS PUBLISHING
All Rights Reserved

Focus Publishing
Post Office Box 665
Bemidji, MN 56619

ISBN: 1-885904-43-6

Printed in the United States of America

Principles

FOR

LIFE CHANGE

From The Pentateuch

To our wives
Christine Williams Hill
and
Kerry Jeanne Horne
for their faithfulness
to God and us

CONTENTS

INTRODUCTION

The Word of God is the believer's all-sufficient resource for all of life and godliness (2 Peter 1:2,3). Often believers limit this resource by studying only a few favorite books in the Bible.

Paul tells us that all Scripture is inspired by God and is profitable. The word "profitable" is translated from a Greek term that literally means "useful." The Word of God was not given to us to merely inform us but to be "used" by us to accomplish God's goal for our lives – that of being transformed into the likeness of Jesus Christ (Romans 8:28,29; Second Corinthians 3:18). Second Timothy 3:16 is the climax of a chapter presenting any and all kinds of problems a believer will face in society or experience in his life. Paul is encouraging Timothy and you that there is an all-sufficient solution — the Word of God. It is all one needs for salvation (v. 15) and sanctification (vv. 16,17).

In v. 16 God gives us a divine four-step order that must be followed to receive the maximum benefit from using Scripture.

Step 1: "Doctrine or Teaching" - This sets the norms for life and godliness.

Step 2: "Reproof" - In this step, erring Christians are rebuked effectively so that the rebuke brings a conviction of wrong.

Step 3: "Correction" - The Greek term means "to set up straight again." After knocking us down, the Scriptures set us up again.

Step 4: "Instruction in righteousness" - This is the idea of disciplined or structured training in righteousness. The Scriptures continue to work in us structuring our lives in daily discipline toward godliness (1 Timothy 4:7).

Another way to see this verse in its four-step order is:

Step 1: The Bible tells us what is right.

Step 2: The Bible tells us what is wrong.

Step 3: The Bible tells us how to get it right.

Step 4: The Bible tells us how to keep it right.

So the Scriptures are all we need to teach us, reprove us, correct us and discipline us toward godliness.

The fact that God's Word is sufficient and "useful" certainly implies that it is relevant to the various questions, concerns, problems, difficulties, conflicts and scenarios of life. As difficult as it may be to believe, it is the opinion of the authors that many believers sitting in church pews of good, fundamental churches have struggled with viewing the Scriptures as the resource to "use" for daily Christian living.

Yes, it gives the message of salvation. And, yes, it teaches you to live, tithe, be kind, stay pure, etc. But does Scripture teach how a wife is to respond to a husband who is a dictator? How is a parent is to respond to a deceptive teenager? How can we be a problem solver when a friend, who is a fellow church member, offends us? What about times when you are overcome with worry, anger or fear? What should you do when a spouse lives one way at home and another way at church? Or when a wife is suspected of extra-marital involvement? What about when a husband is suspected of involvement with pornography? What should you do when your friend at school refuses to speak to you any more because you "stole" her boyfriend? What if you think the coach is not being fair to you?

These, and many other similar scenarios, are where you live day in and day out. The authors' observations, after a combined local church ministry tenure of about 50 years, are that these kinds of situations are either being handled in an unbiblical way based solely on human opinion, in a way that will take the pressure off for the moment, or are not being handled at all.

The commitment of the authors is that God's Word gives clear instruction as to how each believer should think and act in every situation of life. We have been given all we need for "life and godliness" (2 Peter 1:2,3). The Word of God is as current as the very problems you will face today.

To say, in the words of Paul, that the Scriptures are "useful" (2 Timothy 3:16) to "thoroughly furnish each and every believer for every good work" is a real source of hope. God did not leave you to face all that life "throws at you" on your own. He provided an inexhaustible guide to handle all of life's scenarios.

Jesus Christ provides for you a wonderful pattern to follow in the face of temptations, pressures, various struggles, etc. He faced three key categories of temptation that you face:

Lust of the flesh - the desire to experience

Pride of life - the desire to be

Lust of the eyes - the desire to have

Whatever struggle you are having or will have is more than likely included in one or more of these three categories.

At the point of each temptation Jesus Christ "used" the Word effectively. He not only quoted the specific and relevant Scripture, but He responded accordingly. He "used" the Scripture for its intended purpose.

It is interesting that Satan also quoted Scripture. The problem is that he misused it. The misuse was not only in the fact that it was inaccurately quoted, but also in the attempt to inaccurately apply it. Had the Scripture been used for its intended purpose, Christ would have yielded to its authority. When Scripture is taken out of context, misinterpreted, misapplied, or otherwise twisted for purposes other than the Holy Spirit's purpose, it provides no power and holds no authority (in preaching, counseling, or personal use).

The authors' desire is to provide readers with an accurate biblical resource in their pursuit of growth in Christlikeness.

This resource is by no means exhaustive, but can be another "useful" tool in becoming thoroughly furnished for every good work.

One of the initial reasons the authors compiled these principles was to demonstrate to their congregations the practical *usefulness* and *comprehensiveness* of God's Word from Genesis to Revelation. One of the things that adds "usefulness" to this work is that it was born out of pastoral/local church ministry by pastors who are attempting to provide assistance to their flocks for consistent growth into Christlikeness in all areas of life. These principles were not written to merely fulfill the requirement of an academic setting in which a grade was given for memorizing them accurately, but as an aide to help translate *truth into life*. This publication is a by-product of the effort to produce a tool to help people right where they live today.

Paul uses a phrase in Philippians 2:12 that is appropriate and relevant to you as you pursue Christlikeness. He says, "work out your own salvation." Let us be quick to say that what he is not saying is "work *for* your own salvation." The context is definitely a "progressive sanctification" context. He is dealing with the importance of continued obedience to truth in the believer's life. It is an admonition to continue working hard at growth and godliness. As a matter of fact, the word "work" is a present imperative verb. It means a command to do something in the future which involves continuous or repeated action. So Paul says keep on working out your salvation. He gives a huge encouragement in v. 13

when he says that God is working in you, energizing you in the process of obedience.

The strength and power of God are engaged as you step out in obedient living. James puts it this way; the believer who chooses to obey is blessed "in his deed" (James 1:25). As you step out in obedience to God's Word, you too will be blessed, strengthened and encouraged.

"Relevant", "sufficient", "complete", "useful" and "available" are all words that describe God's inspired Word to us. We trust this book will be helpful in putting God's truth to work in your life.

As you are aware, this book covers only the books from Genesis through Deuteronomy, known as the Pentateuch. The authors' goal is to publish additional volumes that will include every book in the Bible.

Bill Hill
Dennis Horne

WHAT IS A PRINCIPLE?

Defining principles in Scripture forces you to be thoughtful and reflective about the text you are reading. It guards you from merely reading a narrative for its literary or academic value. It forces you to see eternal truth being lived out before your eyes and your responsibility to "download" that truth into your own life.

Identifying Scripture causes you to ask important questions about the text:

- What is God doing in this passage?
- What is God teaching about Himself?
- How is He revealing Himself to His people?
- What is God requiring of me?
- What truth is God emphasizing or teaching?
- What eternal truths are being lived out on the stage of this text?

A principle is a biblical truth that is both timeless and universally applicable.

Obviously the principles of which we speak are spiritual or biblical in nature. They speak to the issues of life and godliness. They deal with man's relationship to his Creator- God, and his relationships with his fellow man.

The element that makes a principle cross-generational or timeless, authoritative and practically relevant, is the fact that it is intrinsically connected to and flows out of the character of God and His Word that is forever settled in heaven.

- A Bible principle is **authoritative** because it flows out of a text inspired by God. It is gleaned from Scripture breathed out by God.
- A Bible principle is **timeless** because the nature of Scripture is timeless.

Fundamentally people don't change from one generation to the next. The cultural surroundings may differ with changes in technology, fashion, decorating, fads, etc., but the people (i.e., their ideas, opinions, philosophies, desires, needs, conditions, etc.) don't. The point is that Scripture is equally relevant to each and every generation.

A "principle" that is stuck in a "time warp" is not truly a biblical principle. It may be a reflection of culture at the time. It may be a Bible character's opinion on a subject at the time. It may even be clearly seen in the text. But if it's limited to that person, that culture, or that generation, then it is not an eternal Bible principle by our established definition.

Principles of architecture, design, engineering, boat construction, etc., may be different today than in Noah's day (Genesis 6), but principles of trust, faithfulness, persistence, handling rejection and scorn, believing God despite the majority, etc., are just as relevant today as in Noah's day (Hebrews 11:7).

Principles and strategies of warfare may be different today than they were in Jonathan's day (I Samuel 14). But principles of commitment to God's cause, courage in the face of odds, leadership and perseverence in difficult times are timeless for Jonathan (I Samuel 14) and you.

- A Bible principle is **universal** because it is not limited by or tied to a particular culture, society, geography, age, family, nationality, etc. Biblical principles are equally applicable to all cultures, languages, ages, social classes, etc.

The principle of godly courage needed by a **teenager** (Daniel, Shadrach, Meshach and Abednigo, Joseph, etc.) is no less needed by an **aged man** (Caleb, Paul the Apostle, etc.)

The principle of humility in repentance required of a **prodigal son** (Luke 15:17-19) is no less required of a **king** (Psalm 51).

- A Bible principle is **practically relevant** because the Word of God speaks to every issue of "life and godliness" (2 Peter 1:2,3).

It is the sinful heart of every man that needs to be **redeemed by** Christ (justification) and then **conformed to** Christ (progressive sanctification).

The Word of God provides the truth to address both the penalty of sin and the power of sin.

As the hymn writer put it: "Be of sin the double cure, save from wrath (justification) and make me pure (progressive sanctification)."

Second Timothy 3:15-17 makes it clear that God's Word is able to save (v. 15) and sanctify (v. 16,17).

CRITERIA FOR A BIBLE PRINCIPLE

1. It must be **cross-generational** or **timeless** in nature.

   Eternal truth is applicable regardless of the historical setting.

2. It must be **universal** in scope.

   Eternal truth is applicable regardless of man's culture, language, age, or geography.

3. It must pass the **"unity"** test of hermeneutics.

   The established principle cannot contradict or fight against other non-negotiable truths of Scripture.

4. It must be an **unchanging** truth.

   If it is a true Bible principle it will never need to be altered in order to fit a certain class, generation, age, culture or society of people.

5. It must be **eternal** truth.

   The question is not "Is the particular statement true?" but instead, "Is the statement eternally true?"

   Now, it may be true in the sense that it is something that actually happened in a text such as in Genesis 45:15 which shows Joseph weeping as he and his brothers reconcile. The point is not, did Joseph really weep? The text says clearly that he did. That is true. But can an "eternal truth" (one that is timeless, authoritative, and universal) be established, one that would fit all classes, generations, ages, cultures and societies of people? Can we legitimately force "weeping" into a formula for reconciliation?

6. It must flow **out of the text.**

   The principle must be the product of diligent study and exegetical work that results in an accurate interpretation of the passage. Then based on that effort the wording of the eternal truth can be established. This process is vitally important because the interpretation of the text leads directly to life application.

   For example: Look at Nehemiah 1:4-7:

   And it came to pass, when I heard these words, that I sat down and wept, and mourned certain days, and fasted, and prayed before the God of heaven, ⁵And said, I beseech thee, O LORD God of heaven, the great and terrible God, that keepeth covenant and mercy for them that love him and observe his commandments: ⁶Let thine ear now be attentive, and thine eyes open, that thou mayest hear the prayer of thy servant, which I pray before thee now, day and night, for the children of Israel thy servants, and confess the sins of the children of Israel, which we have sinned against thee: both I and my father's house have sinned. ⁷We have dealt very corruptly against thee, and have not kept the commandments, nor the statutes, nor the judgments, which thou commandedst thy servant Moses.

- What is going on here?
- What is God showing you about Nehemiah?
- What is God showing you about a man in Nehemiah's position?
- Who is Nehemiah?
- Is Nehemiah a leader? How do you know?
- Is he a leader in this text? What is he doing in Shushan the palace?
- What do we learn about Nehemiah from Chapter 2?
- How has God positioned Nehemiah for such a time as this?
- Why does Nehemiah seem to be so concerned about the news he received in 1:2,3?
- Does the fact that he "wept, mourned and fasted" effect the principle you will establish?
- Does the fact that he "sat down" matter?

We could probably go on and on with other questions. But the point is, in order to pull an accurate principle from this text, many, if not most or all of these questions, need to be answered. Now, you may not consciously list and answer each one, but you would need to have a pretty good grasp of the information that these questions would yield.

Having looked at the text and gone through a series of pertinent questions, let's list some "principles." The word is in quotation marks because some of the following statements will obviously not be an eternal truth that flows out of this text or may not flow from the text at all. But we do want to write one that truly fits our established criteria.

"Principles" from Nehemiah 1:4-7:

- A godly leader is an important person.
- A godly leaders cries when he gets bad news.
- A godly leader cries because he is a weak man.
- A godly leader should pray.
- A godly leader should identify with the people he leads.
- A godly leader should go through tough times to see if he's sincere.
- A godly leader tends to be an emotional person.
- A godly leader should listen to people talk about their problems.
- Bad news causes people to cry.
- People should bring bad news to others.
- A godly leader should confess the sins of his people.

Now, could any or all of these be "squeezed" into or "jerked" out of this passage? Could they be forced into the text? Do any *really* accurately reflect the flow and content of the text? Do any of them pass the criteria we laid down?

- Is it true?
- Is it universal?
- Is it timeless?
- Does it flow out of the text?
- Does it apply across the board to kings, commoners, pastors, dads, etc.?

So far we *really* haven't captured what is actually happening in Nehemiah 1:4- 7. Remember, the product of your diligent study and exegetical work should be the accurate interpretation of the passage. Having done that, you can now capture the essence of the passage and clearly state the eternal truth.

Perhaps the best way to "principlize" these four verses is to say it this way:

A godly leader intercedes for his people.

- It passes our criteria in every way.
- It is not forced.
- It is true.
- It is not manufactured or fabricated, but rather reflects what Nehemiah is doing for his people, the Jews.

Now, the specifics of a godly leader's intercession may change. The circumstances that motivate a godly leader to intercede may change.

- It may be a king interceding for his nation.
- It may be a pastor interceding for his congregation.
- It may be a dad interceding for his children.
- It may be a husband interceding for his wife.
- It may be a deacon interceding for his care team.
- It may be a teen interceding for his youth group.
- It may be a choir director interceding for his choir, but,

A godly leader intercedes for his people.

The authors' desire is that your love for, commitment to, and application of God's truth will cause you to worship Him more fully and be conformed to His Son more completely.

How To Use This Book for the Greatest Benefit

Our goal in this chapter is to provide examples of the various ways and contexts in which this book can be used. The examples will not be an exhaustive list and, naturally, there will be some overlap. Hopefully these examples will provide some basic direction as well as stimulate creativity for even more uses.

PERSONAL STUDY GUIDE

This method can be implemented at least two ways:

1. A Single Book Study

The first way you may utilize this method is with a single book study. An individual can begin with any book in the Bible and move through it, meditating on each principle and reading the text from which it was pulled. Obviously, the goal is to understand the principle and how it relates to your life. Every principle may not point out a way you need to change your behavior immediately, but it will always point out a way your thinking must come in line with God's. Some of the questions you may ask as you explore each principle are as follows:

- Where is the principle seen in other parts of the Bible?
- In what way(s) does my thinking need to change as a result of understanding this principle?
- Is there a sin in my life exposed by this principle?
- In what specific way am I practicing this principle?
- How would this principle change the way I handle _____?
- In what way and with whom can I minister this principle?
- What might make it difficult to implement this principle?
- How was this principle developed out of the text?
- What does this principle teach me about God, others, myself, my responsibility to love God and others, etc.

There is space below each principle for answering some of these questions. Writing out your comments and meditations will provide a valuable resource for a long time to come.

As you read through the texts and principles, other questions, specific to that particular principle and text, will be seen that will be helpful in understanding and explaining the principle and its application. For example, Principle 11 in Numbers says, "Personal faith *demonstrated by confession* and obedience is necessary for personal forgiveness and cleansing." The following may be questions or thoughts that could help you in thinking through or discussing this principle:

- What does it mean to confess?

- What might some do instead of confess?

- Is there a difference between confession and acknowledgment? If so, what is it?

- What other passages emphasize "confession"?

- Is confession a willful or emotional issue (i.e., Do you have to "feel" like confessing, or is it a matter of obedience?)?

- Is confession genuine if I'm "confessing" and at the same time planning the next time I'll do that same thing? Why or why not?

- What should my intentions be if I'm truly confessing sin?

Obviously, it would be impossible to write this book in one volume and include a tailored series of questions for each principle. Hopefully, these will serve as a model for your approach to each principle.

2. A Systematic Study

A second way you may utilize this method is with a systematic study. The topical index in the back includes many, if not all, of the principles dealing with a particular subject in this book. You may be struggling with fear, peer pressure, hypocrisy, friendships, etc. The topical index is included to provide you with help in each of these and many other areas of life.

PASTORAL AIDE

Because each category or example represents an individual (pastor, school teacher, etc.), the example of "personal Bible study" would apply as well. The authors have used them in a variety of ways in their own churches.

1. One author used these principles in a brief series of Sunday School lessons in his senior high teen Sunday School class. The

class was broken up into 3-4 small groups. Each team was given a passage of Scripture to read. Each team was to identify the principle in the passage. This method provided a great opportunity to remind the teens of some basic principles of hermeneutics and guide them in formulating these principles by which to live.

2. Both authors used them for an extended series on Wednesday nights; teaching these principles *as compact truth to impact life.* Moving from Genesis to Malachi provided a great way to continually emphasize to their congregations the relevancy, sufficiency, usefulness and comprehensiveness of all the Word of God.

3. One author used the principles to build messages. For example, the principle in Matthew 3:17 which says, "God gave only one model with whom He is well pleased," was used to build a seven-part message series on "What Did Jesus Do?" At least 25 things He did in the gospels were done as a model for believers. The series didn't deal with the miraculous things He did but, rather, the things He did that we are to do. Some of them included:

   - He grew. (Luke 2:52)
   - He prayed. (Mark 1:35)
   - He used God's truth effectively. (Matthew 4:1-11)
   - He sought out sinners. (John 4:3,4)
   - He took time for little children. (Matthew 19:13-15)
   - He served others. (Mark 10:42-45; John 13:4,5)
   - He confronted lovingly and wisely. (Luke 10:39-42)

4. One author used these principles as part of a Bible survey taught in the adult Sunday School class. The author and three of his men taught the series, with each teaching the principles at various times. Handouts were provided as a tool for the class, and interaction between teacher and class was planned so as to make it more of a "workshop" setting.

TEACHER'S AIDE

This book could be used as a Bible curriculum or as a companion to the curriculum. Rather than merely having the student memorize the principle with the corresponding text, the teacher could use it for growth projects.

Ask the student to choose one principle per week that deals with an area in which he needs to grow. This could be easily done from the topical index. Part one of the project would be to meditate on the principle using the type of questions explained under "Personal Bible Study." The teacher may need to help the student be creative with some good, thought-provoking questions. This aspect could possibly form the "academic" part of the student's grade. Part two of the project would be the actual application or "putting to use" the principles for life change. The following procedure could be effective here:

- Is there a change in my thinking and/or behavior that I need to make? Explain.
- Does it involve another person? Explain.
- When do I plan to implement this change?
- In what way(s) do I plan to implement this change?

Part three of this project would be reporting to the class (if appropriate for public knowledge) the process of thinking, meditating and using this principle for change.

Part four might include the teacher holding the student accountable throughout the year for continued change in that area. The teacher would have to keep up with the areas of desired change and possibly meet with the student individually for accountability.

This method would demand work on everyone's part (even more so than a test given, resulting in a grade on the report card) but would be a powerful way to see the "usefulness" and relevancy of God's truth in action. This method gets truth "off the page" (academic) and "into the life" (growth and change into Christlikeness).

PARENT'S AIDE

These principles can be used in a variety of ways in the family. Again, the suggestions under "Personal Bible Study" apply here.

A family could take a principle a week to discuss at family altar time and then practice it during the week. The principles would have to be age-appropriate. Dad and Mom should be willing to get involved. Both parents need to grow as well as be a pattern of growth for their children. For younger children, a chart could be hung on their bedroom wall as a reminder and a sticker could be given for successful practice of the principles. Be careful not to make this just a behavioral exercise. You also want to make sure the children understand that the goal for using the principle should be motivated by a genuine desire to please God, not just get a sticker.

COUNSELING TOOL

The topical index can be used in two basic ways as an effective counseling tool.

First, it can be a rich resource for the counselor as he studies and prepares for his next session. Even though your goal is not to prepare "canned" answers as if there were only a few basic categories of problems, you need to be as prepared as possible to address themes of sin as they surface in the counseling process.

Second, it can be used as a homework project. As specific areas of sin are pinpointed, the counselor can assign corresponding topics for the individual to work on. The counselor can use a combination of his own creative questions along with the questions suggested under "Personal Bible Study" and the type of projects suggested under "Teacher."

One of the fundamental reasons for giving homework projects is to assist the struggling believer in "working out his own salvation" as Paul commands every believer to do in Philippians 2:12. This topical index could be invaluable in helping to do just that.

As we stated at the beginning of this chapter, these are just a few examples of how this book can be used. Each individual, pastor/teacher, parent, etc., using some thoughtful creativity, could come up with many more methods. Hopefully these five will get you started by "priming the pump."

John told some of his converts in 3 John 4, "I have no greater joy than to hear that my children walk in truth." He didn't say his joy was a result of hearing them quote truth but, rather, "walking in the truth."

May God help each of us "use" His Word so that we may "walk in truth."

Notes

How To Pull Principles From The Scriptures

The Scriptures are often given directly in either principle form or command form. When this is the case, the issue is not misunderstanding God's truth but obeying it and applying it to your life.

For example:

Truth stated as principles:

- A short-fused man makes foolish decisions (Proverbs 14:17a).
- A soft answer diffuses a tense situation (Proverbs 15:1).
- A godly man thinks before he speaks (Proverbs 15:28).
- Biblical repentance demands change (Matthew 3:7,8).

Many times Proverbs gives truth this way. It is short, concise and compact truth.

Truth stated as commands:

- Don't go to bed angry (Ephesians 4:26).
- Renew your mind (Ephesians 4:23).
- Love your wife (Colossians 3:19).

The verb tenses in these verses make it clear that the statements are not suggestions but commands for the believer to obey.

So truth stated as principles and truth stated as commands are relatively simple to identify and determine what you must do.

There is, however, a large portion of God's truth that is given to us in narrative form. These are the sections where truth for life is woven right into the fabric of the story. It is not given as simple, compact principles or commands. It must be gleaned by a clear understanding of what is going on in the story. To accomplish this, several questions must be asked:

- What is actually happening in this narrative?
- What is God doing?

- What is God teaching about Himself?
- Is this section connected to the previous section or the section that follows?
- Have the characters been given responsibility? If so, are they fulfilling it?
- What did God say about the characters?
- What eternal truth is being lived out on the stage of this narrative?
- What character qualities are being commended?
- What character qualities are being condemned?
- What actions are consistent with true biblical living throughout the rest of Scripture?
- What is God emphasizing?
- What is the real point of the passage?
- What does God require of me?

In reading through a narrative you might even want to ask, "What is the moral of this story?" As you move through the text, asking questions and asking the Holy Spirit to teach you the eternal truths, keep in mind some basic principles of Bible study - *context and unity*. Context demands you understand what is before and after the passage. Unity demands that the principle you pull does not fight other passages of Scripture.

Be careful about asking: "What does this mean to me?" That is never the priority question. The most important question is "What does it mean?" What it meant then, it means now. Your job is to think it through and see the eternal truth and its relevance to your life today.

Maybe the best way to explain and illustrate how to pull principles from Scripture is to actually go through the process with a passage.

Let's look at 1 Samuel 15:1-28. Read through these 28 verses thoughtfully, asking the questions given earlier. Now, jot down in the space below one or two principles you think are given in this passage.

Principle 1

_____

_____ verse(s) _____

Principle 2

_____

_____verse(s)_____

There are some obvious and necessary facts that you must recognize in order to pull principles from this passage for use in your life.

Fact: God gave Saul a responsibility (v. 3). It was a clear command.

Fact: Saul did not fulfill his responsibility (vv. 8,9).

Fact: Saul did not obey God (vv. 8,9).

Fact: God was displeased with Saul's disobedience (v. 11).

Fact: Saul did "part" of what God required (vv. 8,9).

Fact: Saul lied to Samuel about what he did (v. 13).

Fact: Saul shifted the blame (vv. 15,20,21).

Fact: Saul was a people-pleaser (v. 24). He feared people more than God.

Fact: Samuel rebuked Saul for disobedience (vv. 14,22,23).

Fact: God judged Saul (v. 28).

These are not all the facts in the narrative but enough to illustrate. Based on these facts, what eternal truths, in principle form, can you pull from this narrative?

Principle: God's Word to you is authoritative, and you are accountable for obedience.

Principle: God's Word is clear.

Principle: Partial obedience is disobedience.

Principle: Others cannot be blamed for your failure when the responsibility is given to you.

Principle: Obedience is better than any substitute you can offer.

Principle: Disobedience yields consequences.

I'll stop here.

These are six principles that clearly arise out of this narrative. No Scripture had to be twisted, misused, stretched, misinterpreted or taken out of context to identify these six principles.

As you meditate on God's truth, thinking it through and using some of the questions above, you will begin to come up with your own eternal principles.

Believe it or not, coming up with the principles is the easy part. The challenging part is evaluating your life in light of these principles and making the necessary changes by implementing these truths. As we mentioned earlier, you must get the truths off the page (academic) and into your life (growth and change into Christlikeness).

One way you could begin to "use" these principles is by asking "self-confrontation" questions that flow out of each one.

For example (Using principles 1, 3 and 4 from I Samuel 15):

Principle 1: Am I quick to respond with obedience to God's commands to me? Why or why not? Cite one or two examples.

Principle 3: Do I often find myself looking for ways to "shortcut" responsibility?

Principle 4: Do I have a tendency to blame someone else or at least find someone to share the blame of my failure? Do I hesitate to take full responsibility for my own words and actions?

A Word of Caution

We need to add just a word of caution as to how not to pull principles and what does **not** constitute a legitimate biblical principle. Another caution that needs to be emphasized is the proper use of some basic principles or rules of hermeneutics (these are the principles and methods of how you interpret the Bible).

Let's use the 1 Samuel 15:1-28 passage again. One example of a misused or misapplied principle from vv. 1b,10 would be: "One needs to always be ready to hear the words of the Lord."

First, God doesn't speak today as He spoke then. In the Old Testament God still spoke audibly, through dreams and visions, etc., because His full revelation was not complete. Today we have the entire revelation of God to us. He finished speaking audibly when the book of Revelation was closed. Now He speaks through His inerrant, sufficient Word.

Second, to pull the above principle would imply, if not say directly, that one can still get a message from God apart from Scripture. This idea violates basic laws of Bible study and leaves God's message to us up to personal feelings or opinions.

Another example of a misused or misapplied principle from v.11 would be: "If one is truly grieved at heart, he will demonstrate that by weeping before the Lord all night."

Now there may be some things that do and should grieve you. But to establish a "grief formula" from Samuel's response would be to take things too far. That is not the point of the narrative and is not intended to be an eternal truth that demands application.

You want to be sure that you heed the admonition of Paul to Timothy when he said, "Rightly divide the Word of Truth" or, "handle the Word of God accurately."

Hopefully these brief ideas will serve to give you some helpful direction as you prayerfully read, meditate and pull eternal principles from God's Word. "Use" them for great growth and profit. May God's Word dwell richly within you to the end that you might become more and more like His Son, our Lord Jesus Christ.

"This book of the law shall not depart out of thy mouth; but thou shalt meditate therein day and night, that thou mayest observe to do according to all that is written therein: for then thou shalt make thy way prosperous, and then thou shalt have good success" (Joshua 1:8).

Notes

Principles FOR LIFE CHANGE

From The Pentateuch

GENESIS

1.   God created man to be dependent upon His counsel, even before the fall (1:28-30; 2:15-17).

2.   God has delegated to man the responsibility to take dominion of and manage His creation (1:29).

3.   God created man as a steward (2:15).

4.   The primary purpose of marriage is to solve the problem of being alone (2:18).

5.   God's design for marriage is one man and one woman (2:18-25).

6.   Implicit in God's design for marriage is a new adult relationship with one's parents (2:24).

7.   The believer should not yield to the temptation to question when God has spoken clearly (3:1).

8.   One of Satan's primary strategies is to deny the authority of God's Word (3:4).

9.   Man's tendency is to escape accountability (3:7-10).

10. Man's tendency is to shift the blame when confronted about his sin (3:10-13).

11. Sin brings negative consequences (3:14-20).

12. God made provision for man's sin through a substitutionary sacrifice (3:21).

13. God will accept no substitute for obedience (4:3-5).

14. Man's tendency is to view himself as a victim when reaping the consequences of his sin (4:13,14).

15. The depravity of man's heart is continually being demonstrated by his lack of submission to the authority of God (9:1; 11:4).

16. God's sovereign plans are accomplished (9:1; 11:5-9).

17. God has delegated to man the authority to practice capital punishment (9:6).

18. External benefits should not be the primary criterion in decision-making (13:10,11).

19. Be cautious: sin is progressive if not handled early on (13:12; 14:12; 19:1,30-36).

20. God's method to carry out His plan needs no human manipulation (15:2-4; 16:2-4).

21. God's timing is always perfect (17:21; 18:10; 21:2; 40:23-41:1a).

22. God always does right (18:25).

23. An inconsistent testimony discredits your message (19:14).

24. Your heart is exposed by your actions (19:15, 16,26).

25. You can always depend on God's promises (15:1- 4; 21:1-5).

26. Your love for God may require a willingness to give up something you hold dear (22:9-12).

27. Stewardship is the management of another's possessions (24:2,10).

28. A servant's success depends upon his fulfilling the will of his master (24:1-4,66).

29. "Never sacrifice the permanent upon the altar of the immediate" (25:29-34).

30. Sin patterns could be passed from father to son (12:11-13; 26:7; 27:5; 31:7; 34:13: 37:31).

31. A man reaps what he sows (27:6,20,24; 29:16,23-25; 31:7; 34:13).

32. Guilt and unresolved conflicts breed fear (33:1, 2).

33. Esau illustrates how love refuses to keep a record of wrongs (33:4).

34. Favoritism breeds resentment among siblings (37:4).

35. Joseph illustrates how to overcome evil with good (37:4, 5, 24, 28; 42:25; 43:34; 44:1; 45:1-5; 50:16-21).

36. Man is responsible to please God in every circumstance of life (39:1-4).

37.   Joseph exemplifies stewardship (39:4,6,8).

38.   Dealing with temptation is a constant battle (39:7-12).

39.   Commitment to our ultimate accountability helps keep us pure (39:9).

40. Doing right may result in negative consequences (39:11-20).

41. God may use the circumstances of life to put you in the place of His choosing (41:9-14; 45:5-9).

42. A biblical view of life demands that the believer acknowledge the sovereignty of God (45:4-9; 50:20).

43. It is not man's place to mete out judgment - good or bad (50:15-20).

Notes

40

EXODUS

1.   The spiritual success of God's people is not dependent on sympathetic civil authority (1:7-12a).

2.   When civil authority violates God's authority, man's allegiance must be to God, regardless of the consequences (1:15-17).

3.   The hope of God's people is based on His faithfulness to keep His promises (2:23-24).

4.   Man's usefulness to God is not solely based on his personal abilities (3:11-14; 4:1-13).

5.   The plagues, which served as an attack on the Egyptian gods, demonstrated God's authority (7:15-12:20).

6.   God's provision for redemption, through a substitutionary sacrifice, must be personally applied (12:3-5,13).

7. Man should recognize that deliverance comes ultimately by the hand of God; however, God's sovereignty does not eliminate man's responsibility (12:31-41; 13:3).

8. God does not equip his servant to be a "one-man show." Therefore, he must develop, use, and delegate to men and women various ministry responsibilities (18:13-26).

9. God's law provides the only means by which one can rightly relate to God and man (20:1-17).

10. Numbers should not determine the choices for the believer (23:2).

11. When God gives instructions, He expects complete obedience (25:8-40).

12. God's provision for man's sin is always a blood atonement (30:10).

13. When God's people are enthusiastic about the work of the Lord, it is often demonstrated through their generosity (36:2-7).

LEVITICUS

1. God has determined the means whereby man receives for-
    giveness and cleansing (1:1-2).

2. Since God's complete Word, not man's limited knowledge of
    it, is the standard for the believer's life, ignorance of God's
    Word neither excuses sin nor eliminates guilt (4:2,3,22,27;
    5:17-18).

3. God will not tolerate that which robs Him of His glory (10:1-3).

4.   God desires and makes provision for His people's growth in holiness (11:44-45; 20:7-8).

5.   God intends His people to be uniquely separated from "Gentiles" (18:1-3; 20:24-26).

6.   Partiality in judgment is forbidden by God (19:16).

7.   God always honors obedience (26:1-13).

8.   God always deals with disobedience (26:15-39).

9.   God responds to genuine repentance with mercy (26:40-42).

Notes

NUMBERS

1. Submission to authority, even when the details of the instruction seem trivial, is important (1:54; 2:34).

2. Though His methods have varied, God has always provided direction for His people (9:15-16).

3. Man's discontent with God's provision often results in selfish choices and negative consequences (11:4-9,18-20,31-34).

4.   God's people, following His direction, is the rule rather than the exception (9:17-23).

5.   The fitting response of faith is obedience (13:30).

6.   Circumstances should not affect your choice to obey God (13:31-33).

7. Discontentment is infectious (13:31-33; 14:1-2).

8. Godly leaders are consumed with a cause bigger than them-selves (14:11-19).

9. Avoid presumptuous sin; it may result in severe conse-quences (15:30-36).

10. A true leader demonstrates biblical compassion, even in the face of rebellion, rejection, and personal attack (16:33,41-48).

11. Personal faith, demonstrated by confession and obedience, is necessary for personal forgiveness and cleansing (21:5-9; John 3:14-15).

12. Failure to obey promptly often intensifies the temptation to disobey (22:12,15-17; 23:13,27).

DEUTERONOMY

1. One generation is responsible to teach the next (4:5-10; Judges 2:10).

2. The commitment that God requires of His children is consistent throughout the Old and New Testaments (6:4-5; 10:12; Matthew 22:35-38).

3. Before a parent can effectively teach, he must internalize God's truth (6:6).

4. God's mandate to parents is that they assume the primary responsibility of teaching their children (6:6-9).

5. Deuteronomy 4:6-9 serves as a biblical model for parents in teaching their children.

    The method of communicating truth is teaching.

    The process of teaching requires diligence.

    The opportunities for teaching are both formal and informal.

6. When enjoying the blessing of God, do not forget the God of the blessing (6:10-17: 8:10-16).

7. God's children are not to marry unbelievers (7:3-4; Judges 3:11-15).

8. God is the source of all man's prosperity; therefore, man cannot claim to be self-sufficient (8:17-18; James 1:17).

9. All anger is not sinful (9:19-20; 29:27-28).

10. A just judgment must be impartial (6:18-20).

11. Caution should be taken against insufficient evidence in any controversy (17:6; 19:15-21).

12. By choosing to give firstfruits, the believer acknowledges God as the source of all good things (26:1-11; Exodus 22:29; Proverbs 3:9).

13. Music is an effective vehicle for teaching truth (3:19-22,30; Colossians 3:16).

14. Music is an effective vehicle for communicating truth from generation to generation (32:44-46).

15. God equips His chosen leaders with gifts and abilities commensurate with their responsibilities (34:9-12)

TOPICAL INDEX

Topic	Book		Principle #
Accountability		Genesis	9
		Genesis	39
		Leviticus	2
Anger		Deuteronomy	9
Atonement		Exodus	12
Authority		Numbers	1
	Civil:	Genesis	17
		Exodus	1
		Exodus	2
	God's:	Genesis	15
		Exodus	1
Blame Shifting		Genesis	10
Capital Punishment		Genesis	17
Compassion		Numbers	10
Confession		Numbers	12
Conflicts	Unresolved:	Genesis	32
Confrontation		Genesis	10
Consequences		Genesis	31
		Genesis	40
		Exodus	2
Counsel		Genesis	1
Decision Making		Genesis	18
		Exodus	10
Delegation		Exodus	8
Direction		Numbers	2
Discontent		Numbers	3
		Numbers	7

Topic	Book		Principle #
Disobedience		Leviticus	8
Example		Genesis	30
Faith		Numbers	5
		Numbers	12
Family		Genesis	6
Fear		Genesis	32
First fruits		Deuteronomy	12
Forgiveness	Judicial:	Leviticus	1
Generosity		Exodus	13
Giving		Exodus	13
God's Faithfulness		Genesis	25
		Exodus	3
God's Glory		Leviticus	3
Gratification		Genesis	29
Gratitude		Deuteronomy	6
Growth		Leviticus	3
Guilt		Genesis	32
Heart		Genesis	24
Homosexuality		Genesis	5
Hope		Exodus	3
Impartiality		Deuteronomy	10
Influence		Exodus	10
Instruction		Exodus	11
Judgment		Deuteronomy	10
		Deuteronomy	11
Law		Exodus	9
Leadership		Numbers	8

Topic	Book		Principle #
	Numbers		9
	Deuteronomy		15
Love	Genesis		33
Love for God	Genesis		26
	Deuteronomy		2
Marriage	Genesis		4
	Genesis		5
	Genesis		6
	Deuteronomy		7
Music	Deuteronomy		13
	Deuteronomy		14
Obedience	Genesis		13
	Exodus		11
	Leviticus		7
	Numbers		5
	Numbers		6
Partiality	Leviticus		6
Pleasing God	Genesis		36
Prosperity	Deuteronomy		8
	Deuteronomy		12
Purity	Genesis		39
Rebellion	Genesis		15
Redemption	Exodus		6
Relationships	Man/God:	Exodus	9
	Man/Man:	Exodus	9
	Parent/Child:	Genesis	6
	Genesis		34

Topic	Book		Principle #
		Deuteronomy	3
		Deuteronomy	4
		Deuteronomy	5
		Deuteronomy	14
Repentance		Leviticus	9
Responsibility	Man:	Exodus	3
Revenge		Genesis	35
		Genesis	43
Sacrifice	Willingness to:	Genesis	26
Salvation		Genesis	12
Sanctification		Leviticus	4
Satan		Genesis	8
Scripture		Genesis	7
		Genesis	8
		Leviticus	2
Self-sufficiency		Deuteronomy	8
Separation		Leviticus	5
Service		Exodus	4
		Exodus	8
Sin		Genesis	19
		Genesis	30
		Exodus	12
	Consequences of:	Genesis	11
		Genesis	14
		Numbers	9

Topic	Book	Principle #
Sovereignty	Genesis	16
	Genesis	20
	Genesis	21
	Genesis	22
	Genesis	41
	Genesis	42
Sowing & Reaping	Genesis	31
Stewardship	Genesis	2
	Genesis	3
	Genesis	27
	Genesis	37
Submission	Numbers	1
Substitution	Genesis	12
	Exodus	7
	Leviticus	2
Success	Genesis	28
Teaching	Deuteronomy	1
	Deuteronomy	3
	Deuteronomy	4
	Deuteronomy	5
	Deuteronomy	13
	Deuteronomy	14
Temptation	Genesis	7
	Genesis	38
	Numbers	12
Victim	Genesis	14

Topic	Book	Principle #

Biographical Sketches

Pastor Dennis L. Horne - B.A., M.A.

- Married to Kerry in 1976
- Two children: Joel & Jon
- Local church ministry since 1976
- Senior pastor at Mountain Home Independent Baptist Church in Mountain Home, North Carolina since 1987
- Adjunct Professor of Pastoral Studies at Trinity Baptist Bible College

Pastor Bill Hill - B.A., M.A., M. Min.

- Married to Chris in 1974
- Three children: Joshua, Caleb, & Kara
- Local church ministry since 1976
- Senior pastor at Bethany Baptist Church in Brevard, North Carolina since 1987
- Certified member of the National Association of Nouthetic Counselors
- Adjunct professor of Biblical Counseling at Trinity Baptist Bible college, Tabernacle Baptist Bible College and Seminary and Redeemer Biblical Couseling Training Institute.

Pastors Hill and Horne serve on the executive board of Pastors for Nouthetic Ministry. *PNM* is a fellowship of pastors whose purpose is stated in the following bullet points:

- Produce theologically and exegetically based tools for equipping our people for the work of the ministry.
- Encourage, admonish, and sharpen one another in ministry goals, views, and methodology.
- Give and receive Biblical input in handling counseling sessions and church scenarios effectively and efficiently.
- Fellowship with brethren of like ministry philosophy.
- Discuss contemporary issues from a Biblical perspective.
- Establish accountability in areas of life and ministry.

Both pastors are committed, by the grace of God, to a thoroughly Biblical philosophy of ministry that centralizes the person of Christ as Lord of His church and prioritizes the Scriptures as the believer's all-sufficient resource for life and godliness.

Notes